DISCARDED

Illustrations by Leanne Daphne

Text by Elizabeth Cook

Designed by Nick Ackland

White Star Kids® is a registered trademark property of White Star s.r.l.

© 2022 White Star s.r.l.
Piazzale Luigi Cadorna, 6
20123 Milan, Italy
www.whitestar.it

Produced by I am a bookworm.

Editing: Michele Suchomel-Casey

First printing February 2022

ISBN 978-88-544-1845-5
1 2 3 4 5 6   26 25 24 23 22

Printed in Croatia by Graficki Zavod Hrvatske

The life of Martin Luther King Jr.

I am Martin Luther King Jr. When I was born, the United States was a segregated country. This meant that black people and white people did everything separately. I knew segregation was wrong and believed everyone deserved to be treated equally.

I'm well known for my "I Have a Dream" speech. Come with me as I share my inspiring life story with you. Discover how I went from being a child with a dream to an outstanding leader who made America a better place for all.

I was born on January 15, 1929, in Atlanta, Georgia. I was named after my father, so I am known as Martin Luther King Jr. I had a very happy home life with my father; my mother, Alberta; my older sister, Willie Christine; and my younger brother, Alfred Daniel.

Alberta

Martin Luther King Senior

Willie Christine

Martin Luther King Junior

Alfred Daniel

My father was a minister of a church, just like his father. I grew up listening to lots of sermons! I learned that powerful words can be used to help people understand ideas. I also learned to stand up for what I believed was right and to speak out against what was wrong.

Even as a child, I knew segregation was wrong. I believed everyone should be treated fairly, as my father had taught me. One day, I was playing with my best friend and I was shocked to be asked to leave just because of the color of my skin. That was the day I realized something awful was going on!

My mother explained that this had happened because of racism, and I felt so sad. My childhood experiences of racism played a big role in the type of leader I would become.

When I was 14, I entered a speech competition. I put my anger about the unfairness of separate rules for white and black people into words. Amazingly, I won!

"Let us see to it that. . .we give fair play and free opportunity for all people." -Quote from Martin's winning speech.

However, my happiness was cut short. On the bus home, I was asked to give up my seat for a white passenger. I stood for two hours. I was upset and angry but kept quiet for fear of being arrested. I believed that no one should remain silent or accept something if it's wrong. As I grew up, I planned to fight injustice with the most powerful weapon of all: words.

During my studies at Crozer Theological Seminary in Pennsylvania, I admired the Indian leader Mohandas Gandhi. He had chosen to protest with peaceful demonstrations, not violence. I learned from this and discovered that my writing and speeches were the best ways to change people's hearts and minds.

After graduating from Crozer, I studied at Boston University. Boston was a diverse city with no segregation laws. This was where I met Coretta Scott. We fell in love and were married on June 18, 1953.

In 1954, I accepted a job at Dexter Avenue Baptist Church in Montgomery, Alabama. Although life was better for black people in the North, black communities in the South needed my help. As soon as we arrived, we were reminded of the horrors of segregation. Once again, I had to give up my seat to white passengers and drink from separate water fountains. However, every Sunday I preached about equality and inspired a new sense of hope.

On November 17, 1955, our daughter Yolanda was born.

A few weeks later, a lady named Rosa Parks was arrested for refusing to give up her bus seat to a white person. I discussed her arrest with leaders and we planned the Montgomery Bus Boycott. I asked people not to take the bus again until the law was changed. With the buses empty, the bus company would lose money and make the government listen.

Our plan worked! The U.S. Supreme Court changed the law, making black and white people equal on buses. I was so pleased to have reached our goal peacefully. The Civil Rights Movement was just beginning.

The Montgomery Bus Boycott showed the power of peaceful protests. I met with other ministers and formed the Southern Christian Leadership Conference (SCLC), which was dedicated to fighting for civil rights. I traveled across the country giving speeches about injustice. I asked people to join me on protests for change. Black people and white people marched together to protest against segregation laws. We were often attacked and arrested, but we never fought back with force.

While I was traveling, Coretta was at home with Yolanda. On October 23, 1957, our son Martin Luther King III was born.

In Birmingham, Alabama, the people in power did not want segregation to end. They heard that I was planning a peaceful protest, and they made it illegal for me to protest there. I knew that I would go to jail (and I did), but I had to help.

In jail, I wrote a letter about how bad segregation was. I defended the peaceful protests as a key way to create change. "Injustice anywhere is a threat to justice everywhere," I wrote. My words were powerful. The Birmingham campaign showed America just how bad racism was in the South. When the campaign ended, signs that read "Whites Only" were removed.

By now, we'd welcomed two more children to our family: Dexter in 1961 and Bernice in 1963. My family was growing, along with my determination to push for change. My attention turned to one of the most important cities in the nation: Washington, D.C. President John F. Kennedy introduced a new civil rights bill to Congress. If passed, the law would end segregation in public places forever. My efforts to promote this bill would lead to my most famous speech.

President Kennedy invited me to the White House on June 22, 1963. He said, "It ought to be possible. . .for every American to enjoy the privileges of being American without regard to his race or color." President Kennedy gave his support, and the March on Washington for Jobs and Freedom was planned for August 28, 1963.

Over 250,000 people came to support us, and approximately 80,000 of these supporters were white people. Strangers linked arms. It was the largest showing of racial unity America had ever seen. Here, I gave my life-changing speech. It began with four simple, yet powerful, words: "I have a dream." In that speech I used the phrase "I have a dream" many times to express my hope for a society where blacks and whites lived in harmony.

"I have a dream that my four little children will one day live in a nation where they will not be judged by the color of their skin, but by the content of their character." My words inspired the crowd, the nation, and the whole world.

Three months later, President Kennedy was shot. He'd been assassinated. I was very sad, as he'd supported me and my followers. It was a difficult time for America. However, we kept hoping for positive change.

On July 2, 1964, President Lyndon B. Johnson, signed the Civil Rights Act. I was proud as I stood behind him while he signed the bill. After all the hard work, my words of peace and love, not violence and anger, had created the change we so desperately wanted. The Civil Rights Act made discrimination in public places and businesses illegal. It also made it possible for the government to force public schools to end segregation.

On October 14, 1964, I was awarded the prestigious Nobel Peace Prize. I was only 35 years old! This award is given every year to the person or group who has done something important for world peace. My words of hope, peace, and justice called a nation to change its laws, making them equal for everyone. In my acceptance speech, I announced that I would share the prize and the prize money with the Civil Rights Movement.

Although civil rights had progressed, there was still work to do. I wanted to ensure that black people had the right to vote, so I continued to fight peacefully.

On March 21, 1965, I led a march from Selma to Montgomery, Alabama. The group consisted of blacks and whites all marching together. After five days, we reached Montgomery and the crowd had grown to around 25,000 people!

Our march had a big impact. On August 6, 1965, President Johnson signed the Voting Rights Act. This new law ended the unfair rules that made it hard for black citizens to vote. It was a historic moment for me and the country. It proved again that peaceful protests could be successful.

On April 3, 1968, I was in Memphis, Tennessee, to support black sanitation workers who were protesting because they were not paid the same as white workers. Some people were against change, and I started to receive death threats. However, I wasn't afraid because I believed we'd be successful. In what became my last speech I said, "I want you to know tonight that we as a people will get to the Promised Land."

The next day, I stepped out onto the balcony of my hotel in Memphis. I was shot and I lost my life. I'd been assassinated. People everywhere, regardless of the color of their skin, were sad.

I'm remembered as one of the world's greatest civil rights leaders. After I died, people continued to support my dream. My legacy continues around the world. In America, on the third Monday in January every year there is a federal holiday in my honor. It marks my birthday.

A national memorial was created for me in Washington, D.C. It's called the Stone of Hope. It was inspired by a line from my "I Have a Dream" speech: "Out of the mountain of despair, a stone of hope." As people walk through the large pieces that represent the "Mountain of Despair" and arrive at the "Stone of Hope" statue, they are symbolically moving through the struggle that I did during my life.

Throughout my life, I used my words to touch people's hearts with love and justice, rather than with hatred and violence. Throughout your life, whatever struggles you face, always remember to "meet hate with love."

I hope my extraordinary life will inspire and encourage you to believe in your dreams and to help you create a better world for everyone. There is still work to do, and my dream lives on today. . . a dream of a world where people "will not be judged by the color of their skin but by the content of their character."

He wins a speech competition about the unfairness of segregation.

Martin Luther King Jr. is born on January 15 in Atlanta, Georgia. He is named after his father.

King graduates from Crozer Seminary and enrolls in Boston University.

1929   **1943**   **1951**

1935   **1948**

Martin experiences the shock and harsh reality of segregation early in his childhood.

He studies at Crozer Theological Seminary. During this time, King becomes an admirer of the Indian leader Mohandas Gandhi.

King accepts a job as a pastor at Dexter Avenue Baptist Church in Montgomery, Alabama.

The U.S. Supreme Court rules that everyone is equal on buses. The Montgomery Bus Boycott ends.

1954

1956

1952

1955

He meets Coretta Scott and they marry the following year.

The Kings' first child, Yolanda Denise, is born. Rosa Parks is arrested for refusing to give up her bus seat to a white person. The Montgomery Bus Boycott begins.

President Kennedy is elected. He supports Martin Luther King Jr.'s desire for change.

The Southern Christian Leadership Conference is created. The Kings' second child, Martin Luther III, is born.

King gives his famous "I Have a Dream" speech. A few months later, President Kennedy is assassinated.

1957   **1961**   **1963**

1961   **1963**

Third child, Dexter Scott, is born.

Fourth child, Bernice Albertine, is born. The next month King writes "Letter from Birmingham Jail."

He leads a five-day march from Selma to Montgomery. In August, President Johnson signs the Voting Rights Act.

A federal holiday is created in the United States to honor Martin Luther King Jr. on his birthday.

1965

1983

1964

1968

2011

The Civil Rights Act is signed. Later that year, Martin Luther King Jr. wins the Nobel Peace Prize.

Martin Luther King Jr. is assassinated on April 4 in Memphis, Tennessee.

MARTIN LUTHER KING JR. 1929 - 1965

A national memorial to King, called the Stone of Hope, is dedicated in Washington, D.C.

QUESTIONS

Q1. When was Martin Luther King Jr. born?

Q2. When he was a child, why could he
no longer play with his best friend?

Q3. How old was Martin when he won
a speech competition?

Q4. Which inspiring leader did he admire?

Q5. What was the name of the woman
who became his wife?

Q6. What was the name of the woman who refused to give up her seat on the bus?

_____

Q7. What was the name of the boycott that ended segregation on the buses?

_____

Q8. What was the name of the famous speech that King gave at the March on Washington?

_____

Q9. What award was he given in 1964 for his civil rights work?

_____

Q10. What is the memorial to Martin Luther King Jr. called?

_____

ANSWERS

A1. January 15, 1929

A2. Because of racism and segregation

A3. 14 years old

A4. Mohandas Gandhi

A5. Coretta Scott

A6. Rosa Parks

A7. The Montgomery Bus Boycott

A8. "I Have a Dream"

A9. Nobel Peace Prize

A10. The Stone of Hope